Cryptocurrency

The Definitive Guide To Cryptocurrency Trading Take Control Of The Market With Assurance

(Altcoins To Generate Passive Income Using Successful Techniques)

Jordon Mendez

TABLE OF CONTENT

Moving Forward in the Market 1

How to Use Decentralized Consensus 27

Who oversees server maintenance, and why? 39

Cryptocurrency Faucets 89

Using the Internet to Earn Cryptocurrency Payments 92

Considerations for Cryptocurrencies 93

Ethereum Smart Contracts 112

Moving Forward in the Market

It's time to start getting our hands dirty now that we've studied the fundamentals of the trading system and how to start profiting from FOREX transactions. We're going to look at how you can start acting in the market in this chapter. So, just like when you go live, you may start creating your early tactics.

It's crucial for you to comprehend how the market sets pricing if you're investing in FOREX. As was already said, supply and demand are the driving elements behind the currency market. This implies that both buyers and sellers attend the market with the intention of exchanging goods in order to fulfill their respective needs.

In a typical market, customers arrive well-prepared to make purchases of necessities. When it comes to sellers, they go to the market with the intention of getting money in return for their goods. In FOREX, you simply exchange one currency for another. Although it may seem illogical at first, you are really doing that.

This clearly differs from the stock market, where you trade money for firm shares. However, the FOREX market is quite liquid, which means that there is always a lot of money available. As a result, if you need money, you may rationally liquidate your investment.

You cannot simply do this via the stock market.

Investors in FOREX are quite aware of all the many factors that affect currency value. We spoke about how crucial political, social, and economic developments are to a currency's total worth in the fundamental analysis part. There is no doubt that each of these components is important.

But eventually, each of these components must come together. The price is that point. All the elements that affect how much a currency is worth on the market are reflected in its price. Whether these factors are basic in origin or technical in character, they all work together to generate an influence on pricing. Price here refers to the exchange rates between two different currencies.

Therefore, the focus of this chapter will be on price movement and how you may utilize it to develop your first trading strategy.

Utilizing the Price Action Strategy
"Price Action" in FOREX refers to a discipline that aids you in choosing how to execute deals. The price is the only indication that accurately represents any changes that may be occurring in the market, despite the fact that there are several tools, such as moving averages, that may be used to identify support and resistance levels. This is a crucial factor

to take into account while examining both basic and technological facts.

You must examine the price trend over a certain time period in order to profit from the Price Action technique. Charts created by your trading platform might be used for this. These graphs show price changes based on the statistical device known as a "candlestick." Candlesticks are utilized to calculate both the average and the open and close prices of a pair, as we explained before. This is crucial to remember since longer candlesticks show a wider gap between the open and close prices, whilst shorter ones show a smaller one.

You'll discover that a number of indicators are employed to choose a FOREX strategy. These include the Stochastic Oscillator, the RSI, and the MACD (moving average convergence divergence technique). These metrics aim to simulate price changes. But since they don't consider all that is going on with the pricing, they are often wrong.

The moving average, which displays the average price of a currency pair over a certain amount of time, is maybe the greatest indication outside of the price itself. The final result is a graph showing the average price over time, which demonstrates the price trend of two currencies.

Based on trade volume, the RSI and Stochastic Oscillator are calculated. It might be misleading to use these measurements as your primary source of trade information since there could be a variety of causes for the higher trading volume. Price is thus the sole real, accurate indicator of movement.

Fundamentals of Price Action
You must familiarize yourself with price charts if you want to employ the price action approach as a component of your overall trading strategy. Your platform may produce them for you using whatever timeline you select, as we've already discussed.

Here are some basic principles to remember while using Price Action:

• It's preferable to follow a plan you've started experimenting with as closely as you can. Investors often commit the error of switching between strategies. For example, if you decide to utilize the MACD, stay with it until you have it down. In light of the intricacy of the components involved, this will help you obtain a feel of where this plan will lead you. You'll discover that successful investors begin by perfecting one technique. They may check out other options after they see it can provide them high returns. They may try another if it falls short of their expectations.

• When examining data, pay attention to longer durations as well. A timeframe might be a week, a month, or simply a single day. In a similar vein, you may examine years' worth of data. It is usually preferable to consider longer periods in this situation. You may examine the activity over a month or longer, for example. This aids in removing any irrational trading spikes that could have led you to believe that you were trading too aggressively. This is important to remember since unexpected occurrences might affect investor psychology and cause a surge in trading. This is crucial to keep in mind since excessive trading might backfire. When we say "overtrading," we imply making too many deals quickly. If you focus on shorter timescales, like a week or a few days, you can fall victim to this mistake.

• Copying successful trades is perhaps the simplest method to start learning Price Action. Although it may seem obvious, this really makes a lot of sense. You may develop a feeling of how to decide what to do in each scenario by modeling successful deals. You will be able to devise your own plan as you acquire experience.

Look at daily charts when you first start using Price Action. Patterns may be easily found using daily charts. For instance, you can discover that some currency pairings see more trade activity during particular hours of the day. This may be a reflection of the opening and shutting of other markets. You could also see that buying and selling are triggered by certain price points. Therefore, using these points as a guide, you may choose where to enter.

So let's look at some price action trading tactics that will help you maximize your trades.

Retesting a Broken Trendline Method
This tactic is based on the idea that after the mean has been violated, pricing behavior will return to the mean. This tactic takes use of the fact that, barring large changes, all prices ultimately return to their mean. But changes in mean often take a long period (relatively speaking) and do not occur immediately.

Plotting a trendline for any currency pair is required for this Price Action method. The trendline should, in general, include at least 20 time periods (often a greater duration like an hourly chart). You may thus look at the changes during the last 24 to 48 hours. You should have adequate knowledge from this on the general pattern of the pricing itself.

Then, you may search for instances when the price of the currency pair really breaks the trend and trades above or below the trendline. When this happens, you may anticipate that the price will resume following its initial pattern. Here is where you may bet on making money. Furthermore, you may anticipate that the price will ultimately return to the area where you first saw it with some degree of accuracy.

You may review earlier times when the value of the currency pair violated the trendline to double-check your plan. In these circumstances, you must research how long it takes for the currency pair to trend again. In certain cases, it can just take a few hours. In other cases, it might potentially take several days. At the end of the day, a lot will rely on the state of the market. However, past actions should give you a pretty clear idea of what to anticipate.

This method doesn't need any unique signs to be effective. In actuality, all you need is a price chart with at least hourly data. However, you should avoid looking at shorter timescales, like daily data, since you can miss a lot of information. An hourly chart with a history of around 24 to 48 hours is a suitable starting point.

Levels of Resistance and Support
You must concentrate on the support and resistance levels, as shown in price patterns, in order to make the break and retest approach effective. A support level is essentially the lowest point at which the price will fall before rising again. In contrast, a resistance level is the

maximum level that a price will reach before declining.

You can tell the range in which a currency pair is trading by glancing at these levels. As a result, you can forecast how low and how high a price will go. In general, you may find these spots by analyzing the price movement during the previous 24 to 48 hours.

Keeping an eye on resistance and support levels and hitting them at least three times in a row is a decent rule of thumb. You may presume that any divergence of these support levels will indicate a reversion to mean when you see that the actual figure of a support or resistance level is always the same, even when it is extremely near.

Assume you are keeping an eye on the USD/EUR pairing. You see a level of support at one and a degree of opposition at one and five. This suggests that this range will be the trading range for this combination. You note that the low point has reached 1, or is very nearly there, during the time period you are studying. When this level is reached, the price returns up to a maximum of 1.05. The price will then return all the way to 1 before rising again. When you have seen this behavior at least three times, you may infer that each time the price crosses one of these boundaries, a return to the mean will occur.

Tracking the price movement over a certain time period is hence where you may put the approach into practice. You should keep an eye out for the price breaching either the support or resistance level when you observe the price touch one of them. You may set up your trade to execute as soon as the price crosses either threshold. Your entrance point may be either above or below the break, and your exit point can be when the price returns to its mean.

A word of warning: use this technique with caution when there is a significant level of volatility, as seen by sharp fluctuations in price or trading volume. In these circumstances, you can see extraordinary price movement that takes longer than anticipated to return to the mean.

Candlestick pattern with engulfing bars
As part of this technique, we'll examine how candlesticks may be used to track price movement and perhaps spot reversals. When trying to keep track of entrance and departure locations, this tactic is quite helpful. Generally speaking, you monitor price movement over a certain length of time in order to predict the point at which the price of a currency pair will change trend.

An upward or downward trend is one of two patterns.

A rising price trend is referred to as a bullish trend. As a result, you may anticipate that the reversal will signify a negative trend. Generally speaking, you want to follow the trendline as it approaches the maximum point of the resistance level. When this occurs, it is anticipated that the trend would return to the mean.

The downward price movement is referred to as the bearish trend. As a result, you anticipate the reversal to see price movement rising again. In general, you're trying to pinpoint the precise location when the trendline crosses the resistance level's lowest point before turning around.

The candlesticks follow the trendline in each of these methods to show when the real reversal has occurred.

Follow the trendline to its lowest or highest point to get the precise location. You'll see a candlestick that is quite short. When the next candlestick is much bigger than the preceding one, a reversal has officially occurred. As a result, the subsequent candlestick "engulfs," or totally hides, the preceding one.

Consider a bearish trend. The trendline is now heading downward in this instance. You can have an anticipation of where the support level might be if you have been following the market activity for some time. The candlesticks will seem to be growing shorter and shorter as you watch the trendline move approaching the support level. Thereafter, you will see a massive candlestick shortly after a very short one. This is the flip-side. The candlestick that is engulfing is this. This may be used as a starting point for a deal.

Let's now consider a bullish trend. You are seeing the peak of the trend in this instance. In essence, you are trying to find an escape point. That is the level of resistance when the trendline reaches its highest point. Every candlestick will seem to be becoming shorter and shorter. The smallest candlestick will eventually be quickly followed by one that is significantly longer and engulfs the first. This is the designated point of reversal and ought to be your departure.

The point of the shortest candlestick is where you should ideally close the position. The maximum point you could possibly reach before your profit starts to decline is this. Even while pinpointing the precise moment of reversal is almost hard, getting as near as possible will help you increase your winnings.

Please take notice that most trading platforms utilize green candlesticks to indicate a bullish trend and red candlesticks to denote a bearish pattern. This color-coded approach is particularly helpful in teaching you how to recognize trend reversals.

Risk Control Using Price Action
Any kind of investment requires effective risk management. By adhering to tried-and-true risk management procedures, you can protect yourself against errors that might result in the loss of all of your investment cash.

So let's look at some risk management principles you may use if Price Action is your primary FOREX investing method.

• Be on the lookout for instability
The Price Action strategy's main adversary is volatility. It's crucial to remember that when employing price action as your primary investing technique, significant volatility might result in odd swings in price action. You may rationally anticipate that this will occur eventually since prices always have a tendency to return to the mean. However, prices may revert to mean sooner or later than expected when there is a significant level of volatility. As a consequence, even if it is not required, you must keep an eye on this signal.

• Be on the lookout for misleading signals
You sometimes get misleading reversal signs. For example, you could see an engulfing candlestick before the trendline reaches the anticipated level of resistance or support. Although this is

totally feasible, take caution since it can just be the product of an unusually high trade volume. Watch out for confirmation if you identify a potential reversal long before projected levels. Investors that invest right now can get a surprise outcome.

• Request confirmation at all times
If there are any doubts about a signal, always seek confirmation. It would be better to wait for a confirmation if you see a probable reversal that does not follow the typical trading patterns. If a new support or resistance level could exist, confirmation is required. Three hits in a row might act as confirmation of a new level. Some investors only predict a third hit after the first two hits. You may wait until two hits have been made before assuming the third hit if you are more risk-tolerant.

• Exercise caution while investing against the trend.
It is better to stay away from countertrend investing when you are

just starting out. The biggest disadvantage of this strategy is that you predict reversals at times when there may be little technical data to justify them. You could act on a hunch or as a consequence of seeing candlesticks being consumed. Still, you must thoroughly research this dangerous sort of investment.
So how exactly does it all work?

The Ecosystem of Cryptocurrencies

We will examine the fundamental principles that underpin every cryptocurrency in this chapter. As it is, there are several variants on the market, so understanding the basic principles around which they are all built is beneficial. Be sure to take your time reading through the various parts if you're new to this technology. Where references are needed for further comprehension, links have been supplied.

Describe Blockchain.

Let's start by asking ourselves why we need money in the first place. In order to give something to someone else (purchasing) or take something from someone else (selling), we need money. Is this not correct? That's when a blockchain enters the picture for a cryptocurrency. Blockchain is a system that enables safe bitcoin transfers between users. All transaction records are kept in a distributed database. The blockchain of a cryptocurrency is disseminated and extended across several nations and people, unlike a traditional fiat money. A peer-to-peer network is maintained by volunteers who also manage the databases and servers. There is no chance that the government or any other entity will interfere with the database records. Even if hostile parties or government officials volunteer to maintain the blockchain, they are unable to change the transaction records because of the limitations imposed by its architecture.

In essence, a blockchain is an open electronic ledger with all transactions visible to the public. The most recent Bitcoin transactions, for instance, may be accessed at https://blockchain.info/. Blockchain's open architecture eliminates fraud and counterfeiting. You can confirm that the transactions are entirely valid by reviewing the blockchain. A transaction you perform will soon be visible on the public blockchain.

But won't people be able to see who is spending how much by looking at the blockchain, you could be asking. The answer to that is no since encryption and mapping tools are used to secure your identify. The only item that will show up on the blockchain will be your Wallet-ID, which is completely anonymous. Later in this chapter, we shall discuss a cryptocurrency wallet's workings.

Why do people mine?

We need to know how the blockchain gets updated universally throughout the network now that we have a basic understanding of what it is. It must be agreed upon by all nodes since otherwise there would be differences in transaction verification, which will eventually lead to fraud and system collapse. Let's investigate this in more depth now.

In a blockchain network, nodes come in two different varieties. Mining nodes and common nodes. Both of them have unique functioning procedures of their own. Additionally, each node manages a unique blockchain that is built by separately adding valid blocks to the list. The functioning of the typical nodes is rather simple. Their responsibility is to validate the transactions and transmit them forward to the other nodes after receiving transaction-messages from nearby nodes in the network. By doing this, it will be made sure that only legitimate transactions propagate across the network over time. This serves as a fundamental layer of security to prevent the blockchain from being updated with fake transactions.

The mining nodes are now a distinct class of nodes that carry out the mining protocol, which entails the following processes.
Pay attention to any new transactions, then confirm them.
→ Verified transactions should be combined into a block. Create a Proof-of-Work method for that particular block, calculate its solution, timestamp the block and the result, and send it out through the network.

In essence, the mining nodes aggregate fresh, legitimate transactions into blocks and distribute them to other nodes. Any node may evaluate the block's validity by looking at the proof-of-work value. Therefore, when the remaining nodes get this new block, they verify its authenticity and add it to their own blockchain. The mining node that sent the legitimate block with the earliest timestamp receives a reward. This prize typically consists of a certain number of bitcoin units. The processing fee levied by banks and other financial institutions is comparable to this.

Now that we understand how blocks are created, how the blockchain works, and how the Proof-of-Work protocol ensures that every node on the network understands the blockchain, we can better understand how blocks are mined. Here's when things gets interesting. The majority of cryptocurrencies, including Bitcoin, only allow for the creation of new coins via mining. That is to say, measuring the amount of computing done by the mining nodes is the sole method for the system to determine the value of the coin. Every single bitcoin that has ever been "minted" was produced by a mining node using the Proof-of-Work algorithm to generate a fresh valid block.

Therefore, mining serves two purposes. to produce fresh money and add legitimate transactions to the blockchain. To encourage them to carry out the required calculations, miners are compensated. There wouldn't be enough miners to swiftly verify the transactions if there was no incentive. Due to its significant latency, this would result in a system that is relatively risky. The speed at which transactions are checked affects the cryptocurrency's security. And it depends on how many miners are concurrently vying for the payout. This is the elegance of the blockchain-based bitcoin system. Additionally, the bitcoin system's mining incentive decreases by 50% every four years. In the end, the transaction fee and tips would be the only compensation for mining blocks. This is a means to make sure that the cryptocurrency's value doesn't fall below a specific level as a result of its restricted supply.

How to Use Decentralized Consensus

The blockchain's design makes it unnecessary to have a central database or oversight organization. You must realize that this is a revolutionary technical shift that affects not just the world of digital currency but also those of business, finance, government, politics, etc. The ability to create a system like bitcoin that reaches decentralized agreement in a safe and effective way has opened up a wide range of opportunities. Due to this invention, new self-verifying systems and decentralized applications are now being created.

For those who are not familiar, decentralized consensus is when a network of entities comes to a shared understanding without having to rely on one another (in our example, the legitimacy of a transaction). A significant area of study in the science of distributed systems is what is often referred to as distributed trust-less consensus. To address the issue of distributed consensus, several methods have been developed. As we've seen, the Proof of Work (POW) protocol is used by cryptocurrencies like Bitcoin to enable widespread consensus and unaffected operation of the blockchain network. It's crucial to comprehend why reaching distributed consensus in a cryptocurrency's blockchain network is so crucial.

Assume for the moment that you have a loosely linked network of computers (often referred to as "nodes"). The backbone of your service is made up of this network. In other words, this network manages all compute and database storage tasks in the background. Your goal is to make sure that every activity a user does must be tracked and updated consistently throughout the network. Because of this, you must portray a single, consistent experience to users everywhere even while your network is spread. This is the most fundamental need for practically every technological business in existence, including Google, Facebook, Amazon, Instagram, and others, as well as for a cryptocurrency like bitcoin.

You will see that when a user takes an action, you are invariably left with only two possibilities in order to fulfill the goal of consistency. Either log this activity in every node or none at all. If you just record it in a few nodes, the network becomes inconsistent and the nodes are unable to determine if the user really carried out the activity or not. To put it another way, the network is unable to reach a consensus. An inconsistent network is an unsecure network, hence this is a major issue. This contradiction might be used by any hacker to disseminate viruses or change the database to their own ends. As a result, maintaining consistent data across all nodes and having rapid access to erroneous and inconsistent information are crucial for distributed networks. This is why decentralised consensus in a blockchain network is so crucial.

Let's now examine how the blockchain specifically helps to achieve this decentralized consensus. Bitcoin will be used as our standard cryptocurrency.

A blockchain's decentralized consensus is very fantastic. This is so that every node in the network may concur that a transaction is genuine without having to rely on one another or know who the parties are. It also goes by the name of "trust-less decentralized consensus" for this reason.

Blockchain-based cryptocurrencies use emergent consensus to create decentralized control. This indicates that there is never a single moment in time when every node in the network may concur that a transaction is genuine. More nodes will eventually be able to reach the same conclusion as time goes on.

This emergent distributed agreement is attained via four stages. Let's take a careful look at them.

Phase 1: Each node must verify each incoming transaction.

The network's nodes get information about different transactions from nodes that are close by. Simply said, some of these transactions are invalid. Therefore, as a general rule, each node examines the incoming transactions and gathers the legitimate ones into a mempool or transaction pool. Using cryptographic methods and a set of openly available criteria, the transactions are confirmed.

Each node propagates this pool of legitimate but unconfirmed transactions across the network. Thus, the network's nodes eliminate all incorrect transactions.

Phase 2: Mining nodes build blocks of legitimate transactions.

As we saw earlier, mining nodes are specialized nodes in the network whose task it is to gather legitimate transactions from their nearby nodes, group them into a block, and then calculate an exclusive value (the "Proof of Work") for the block using a cryptographic method. The mining nodes maintain track of the most recent blocks and compete with one another to produce a fresh block containing these legitimate transactions and the necessary proof-of-work. These blocks are then sent to other nodes on the network.

Nodes receive and validate blocks in phase three.

The nodes in the network determine the authenticity of blocks as they are received from different mining nodes. Transactions may be accumulated into blocks by anybody. The secret, though, is in how difficult it is to calculate the exact "proof-of-work" of a block, which lowers the likelihood of transaction fraud.

When the nodes get a block from a mining node, they check it against the "proof-of-work" and add it to the blockchain they have been up-to-date with.

Phase 4: Nodes remove unnecessary blocks

Every node updates and maintains its own blockchain, which is effectively a list of blocks that have been verified using widely acknowledged standards. Multiple legitimate blocks may be sent to nodes by various mining nodes. So how can they determine as a group which of the received blocks should be taken into account for expanding the blockchain? The proof-of-work mechanism is useful in this situation. The proof-of-work values for various blocks vary. According to the Bitcoin protocol, the blocks with the greatest proof-of-work value should be chosen first. A node will thus keep two distinct lists in the blockchain if it receives two different blocks until one of them outweighs the other in the overall cumulative proof-of-work value sum. The sub-chain with the lowest proof-of-work value total will then be discarded. Because the proof-of-work value total is a measurement of the amount of computing performed by the mining nodes, the nodes in a sense favor the sub-chain in which they have invested more processing power.

The Issue of Double Spending

Bitcoin creator Satoshi Nakamoto was the first to introduce the idea of a blockchain. Because it was able to do what no other digital currency did at the time—ensure that the cryptocurrency units cannot be spent more than once—it was (and still is) regarded as a technical marvel. The issue of double spending is what this is known as.

In contrast to fiat money, the production of currency units is not a difficulty with virtual money. Anyone is free to develop protocols or algorithms describing the creation of virtual currency units, their structure, the size (in bytes) of each unit, and other requirements. However, Double Spending is the underlying issue that all currencies, particularly digital currencies, must address.

A double-spend occurs when one piece of money is used in two different transactions. The unit itself may be copied or the transaction record can be altered to do this. This 'record' in the context of cryptocurrency is the blockchain ledger. The double-spending issue is resolved in a normal fiat currency by using unique methods to produce money and spot counterfeit notes. The banks that handle fiat currency transactions also use stringent security procedures to guard against hacking and hijacking of their databases, which include all of the transaction and account information. The potential for harm is enormous if the bank's computer network's security was breached. The double-spending issue cannot be solved by a fiat currency, as seen by the many instances of bank fraud, hacker attempts, and cash duplication.

So how does something like bitcoin, a cryptocurrency, handle this?

A system like bitcoin does not preserve the "balances" of the people, unlike a centralized fiat money. It simply keeps track of a blockchain, or ledger of transactions. Therefore, the only way to solve this problem is to give each bitcoin a unique identification. This way, if someone attempts to spend a bitcoin twice with the same identity, they can compare it to previous transactions in the blockchain.

When you transfer someone bitcoins, the transaction is tracked and recognized using a UTXO, or Unspent Transaction Output, which is how it all works. This UTXO is the distinctive identifier for a bitcoin transaction, which is comparable to a bill of conventional money. UTXOs can only be used as wholes. However, they may be split up into a number of smaller UTXOs to facilitate transactions.

To produce the new set of UTXOs you need to spend some bitcoins, you must either combine or divide two UTXOs. Consider, for instance, that you have two UTXOs, each worth 0.3 and 0.6 bitcoins, from Alice and Bob, respectively. These will be referred to by their IDs, X and Y. Therefore, X stands for Alice's UTXO and Y for Bob. Let's assume that you wish to transfer Carter 0.7 bitcoins. This is how the conversion works:

Z(0.7 bitcoins) + W(0.2 bitcoins) are obtained by adding X(0.3 bitcoins) and Y(0.6 bitcoins).

In order to provide Carter 0.7 bitcoins, two new UTXOs with distinctive IDs Z and W were created. Now, Carter's signature must be used together with this new UTXO(Z) in order to be utilised. It spreads over the network before being gathered by a mining node, who then hashes it into a block and updates the blockchain. The transaction is carried out in this manner. Additionally, a program known as the cryptocurrency wallet, which we'll examine later in this chapter, manages the conversion. The other UTXO(W), worth 0.2 bitcoins, is returned to your wallet and may only be spent when accompanied by your signature.

With this setup, all a node has to do to determine if a bitcoin is being "double-spent" is to compare the UTXO ID to the blockchain's transactions. Even if a node's blockchain is only partially complete, the flawed UTXO will only go so far before being rejected by other nodes with fully verified blockchains.

Who oversees server maintenance, and why?

You may be thinking who would want to maintain and update the blockchain if it requires so much work. Who would want to volunteer for a situation like this?

Incentive programs for mining are the solution. As we've previously seen, the majority of cryptocurrencies are created in a method that rewards users with new crypto-coins for validating transactions and maintaining the blockchain. This provides them the motivation to put up the effort. The only viable method for sustaining a distributed, decentralized bitcoin network is to compensate the miners. This is due to the fact that mining crypto-coins costs a lot of money and demands a lot of processing power from specialized GPUs.

Additionally, as mining is the only means to produce cryptocurrency, fresh crypto-coins are only produced when a miner adds a new valid block to the network. This is a brilliant method for resolving two issues simultaneously. The network receives fresh crypto-coins to operate with, and the miners are rewarded.

It is crucial that the system be set up such that anybody may join and offer to work as a miner in the network. If mining was only available to a select few, banks, the government, or the top 1% could be able to gain excessive influence over the system. The security and decentralization of the coin may be compromised as a result. Customers would be in difficulty, for instance, if a bank was bombed and/or its systems were compromised. But there wouldn't be a single weak link in a vast network of mining volunteers. When creating the system framework, Satoshi Nakomoto took care to take this into account.

What makes it safe?

Let's concentrate on just one cryptocurrency — bitcoin — in order to provide an answer to this topic. The world's most popular cryptocurrency is bitcoin. Every day, millions of individuals closely monitor the bitcoin network. Public upgrades to the program are released on a regular basis. According to a 2013 Forbes report, the worldwide processing power of bitcoin is 256 times more than that of the top

500 supercomputers in the world. That ought to give you an idea of how many servers the bitcoin volunteers are managing. Therefore, at this moment, the only methods for hacking bitcoin are to shut down the internet or break the SHA256 algorithm. Of course, this has to do with the architecture of the whole bitcoin network. If you use your wallet without taking the required security precautions (explained later in the chapter), you risk having your bitcoins lost or stolen.

After that, let's examine the likelihood that the SHA256 will be broken.

The cryptographic hash algorithm SHA256 is one that we learnt about in chapter 2. This implies that there is relatively little resemblance between two outputs for two comparable inputs. When a hacker can take a block of transactions, change it somehow, and still get a hash result of 256 bits, we may state that SHA256 has been broken in the context of a cryptocurrency. In this manner, the nodes won't be able to detect the hack when they attempt to validate the hash value of the updated block. Let's now examine the precise steps a hacker would take to accomplish this.

Let's use the letters OB, OH, and MB to denote the original block, the modified block, and the original hash value.

The hacker's challenge is to locate an MB in such a way that:

MB) = OH for SHA256.

OH contains 256 bits, as far as we know. We are aware that a bit may take one of two potential forms: 1 or 0. This indicates that the SHA256 function's result has a potential value range of 2256. However, because SHA256 is a cryptographic hash function (which generates random outputs for two comparable inputs) and not simply any function, the only way to get a desired result is to loop through all feasible inputs and somehow end up with the same output hash as OH. Additionally, since OH contains 256 bits, the hacker must often iterate through 2256 inputs in order to locate a potential match. Let's now acknowledge the complexity of this endeavor. The YouTube user 3blue1brown has a video where they artistically explain this. You should watch it since it's a pretty nice animated video. This is the main idea:

2³² is multiplied by itself 8 times to get 2²⁵⁶.

So 2²⁵⁶ = 2³² * 2³² * 2³² * 2³² * 2³² * 2³² * 2³² * 2³²

2³² is worth around $4 billion.

Therefore, 2²⁵⁶ is (4 billion) * (4 billion) *(4 billion) *(4 billion) *(4 billion) *(4 billion)

Less than 1 billion hashes can be performed per second by a decent GPU. Imagine building a customized computer or server with four of these GPUs that can process 4 billion hashes per second. The first 4 billion factor of 2²⁵⁶ is now taken care of. Let's say you are able to get 4 billion of these specialist computers. For context, consider that Google, the largest search engine and perhaps the most popular website on the internet, only has around 900,000 servers in its data centers. A million is equal to four billion. The first two components of 2256 can thus be handled if you can somehow get 4000 times as many machines as Google does. There are still six more components missing. Assume that everyone on earth has their own personal server farm of 4 billion specialized hash machines in order to handle another 4 billion factor. There are around 7.442 billion people on the planet, thus the third component is no longer an issue.

There are still five aspects to consider. How are they handled? Let's suppose you have contact with extraterrestrials and are able to access the 4 billion planets that are home to 4 billion extraterrestrials, each of whom possesses 4 billion sophisticated computers. The fourth component is now taken care of. The halfway point has come. There are just 4 left. Imagine a universe made up of 4 billion galaxies, each with 4 billion planets. Only three additional elements remain. Scaling using computing resources has been tested. Let's now attempt to scale with time. 126.8 years are equal to 4 billion seconds. 507 billion years, or 4 billion times that, is thought to be 37 times as old as the universe itself. We still have one more element to consider despite that.

Conclusion: If everyone on Earth were to use 4 billion specialized computers, and if there were 4 billion such earths in a galaxy and 4 billion such galaxies, it would take them 37 times as long as the universe has existed to calculate only a fraction of the 2256 possible outcomes, or 1/232. While I can't speak for you, I find it to be rather unbelievable. So, certainly, I would wager on SHA-256's security.

Now that we are aware of how difficult SHA256 is to break, it is critical to comprehend the distinction between safety and anonymity in the context of cryptocurrencies. The fact that SHA256 is difficult to break simply serves to highlight how implausible an assault on the blockchain or the theft of your cryptocurrency would be. It does not, however, imply that you are a completely anonymous user of the system. One of the greatest myths surrounding bitcoin and other cryptocurrencies is this one. Your identity is not completely concealed, but your bitcoins are protected.

The majority of cryptocurrencies, including Bitcoin, only provide partial anonymity. Despite the fact that your identity is kept a secret, the transaction details are updated on the blockchain, which is available to everyone. On the basis of the information from the public blockchain, one may begin to make connections between your activities and your IP address (which is effectively your online identity). To disguise your IP address, you may now use programs like Tor or VPN, however even Tor does not completely provide anonymity. Eventually, a committed hacker with sufficient resources can find your IP address. However, he or she won't be able to take your crypto-coins or mess with them. Having said that, Zcash is the most anonymous cryptocurrency available, so if you're still uneasy I'd advise you to use it. A supplementary program called the wallet is used to provide more secrecy, making it easier for bitcoin users to deal securely. Let's see how it works.

digital currency holder

A digital wallet for your cryptocurrency (like bitcoin), often known as a crypto-wallet, is required in order to conduct transactions. It maintains your bitcoin transactions by communicating with the blockchain, storing your private and public keys, and keys. Without a wallet identity, a bitcoin cannot exist. Every bitcoin unit has to be connected to a wallet and used for transactions. Without the wallet, you cannot spend your cryptocurrency. Additionally, you are unable to spend the same cryptocurrency from several wallets since it conflicts with the blockchain's record.

You may use a variety of wallet kinds. Below is a picture of a mobile wallet, which is simply a smartphone app that organizes your transactions and saves your public and private key information. The particular screenshot was captured from the Google Play Store's Bitcoin Wallet app. Other wallet frameworks include desktop applications, internet wallets (websites), hardware wallets (USB drives, hard drives, etc.), and paper wallets (keys written on a sheet with a QR code).

What's the wallet's mechanism?

A crypto-wallet stores three essential values. the number of cryptocoins, the private key, and the public key. As we've seen, a wallet's main function is to make bitcoin transfers easier. The method is as follows.

Say you wish to give your buddy some bitcoins. The transaction message will be generated by your wallet together with the quantity of bitcoins you wish to transfer and signed (encrypted) using both your private key and your friend's public key. Then, your buddy receives this communication over an internet network channel. By decrypting the message using his private key and your public key, your friend's wallet will be able to determine whether it was indeed sent by you and was meant for him.

Your friend's wallet adds more bitcoins to its holdings and responds after the legitimacy has been confirmed and any chance of a middleman has been ruled out. Your wallet reduces the amount of bitcoin you have after it has received the answer.

To guarantee that the balances in the two wallets relating to a transaction are accurately adjusted, a particular wallet protocol has been put in place. This protocol must be followed by anybody who wants to create their own wallet software, or else the transactions won't be handled.

The blockchain is updated with the transaction record when the balances in both wallets are changed. The blockchain network needs some time to verify the transaction. If everything goes according to plan, the ledger advances; if not, the wallets are notified of a system mistake, and the modification is undone. The standard wallet use-case scenario is now complete.

Many specifics have been left out for the sake of simplicity. Please check the official Bitcoin developer handbook to get more details about this subject.

Security Procedures for Bitcoin Wallets

Your bitcoin will be *TOTALLY LOST* if you lose the wallet or the keys. It could be useful to read about the well-known true tale of James Howells, who unintentionally tossed his old hard drive into the garbage can while cleaning up his desk and lost 7500 bitcoins, which are now worth $19.6 million. According to reports, the hard disk is now four feet under the surface of a Newport landfill. Therefore, there should be no doubt that your wallet's security should come first while working with cryptocurrencies. Here are some pointers to remember.

First tip: You may choose a separate wallet program for every coin. To prevent security and functionality difficulties, please only use wallets that have received official recognition. To determine what is ideal, spend some time looking over the wallet's characteristics and the website for your coin. All the suggested bitcoin wallets may be found at https://bitcoin.org/en/choose-your-wallet for bitcoin.

Tip #2: Make several copies of your wallet's private key and encrypt them before storing them in safe places (both online and offline). Make sure you have at least one copy on hand in a tangible, accessible location, such as a flash drive or a hard drive.

Tip #3: If you have a significant quantity of bitcoin, it is advised to spread out any potential harm by using numerous wallets. Use multisig transactions or two-step verification techniques.

The Most Popular Cryptocurrencies in Chapter Two

We're going to examine the most popular and widely used cryptocurrencies in this chapter.

Bitcoin

The first cryptocurrency to appear was bitcoin, which is now the most popular cryptocurrency. Satoshi Nakamoto created this money, which became available to the general public (online) in 2009. Due to the enormous progress it has achieved since being introduced on the Internet, it is sometimes referred to as the "people's currency". As the decentralized peer-to-peer payment network that it is designed to be, the payment network is driven by its users. When it comes to transactions that take place in Bitcoin, there are no intermediaries or higher authorities. Because Bitcoin is "mined" and used for transactions online, many think of it as Internet currency.

Like no one person has exclusive custody of the technology behind email, there is no particular controller of the Bitcoin network. Bitcoin is controlled by its users worldwide. Developers may try to make the program better, but they can't compel the software to modify its protocol. As long as it abides by the requirements connected to the original program, users have the option to choose the version of Bitcoin they would want to use. All users and developers have a strong motivation to keep this agreement safe as a result.

From the standpoint of the user, Bitcoin is only a software or application that gives users the ability to conduct transactions between their wallets. The main difference is that users now send and receive bitcoin rather than conventional cash. It doesn't take a lot of knowledge to achieve it. This is how cryptocurrency works for the majority of people.

People often believe that it is difficult to make Bitcoin payments, yet this couldn't be farther from the reality. Compared to using a credit or debit card, bitcoin payments are simpler to make. Additionally, doing so is far less expensive. Bitcoin payments may be made on a computer or a standard smartphone as long as the necessary wallet application is installed. Simply input the recipient's address, the payment amount, and submit the transaction to complete the payment. Wallets may read recipient addresses from QR codes or by using NFC, which is a commonly used technology on the majority of smartphones.

Ethereum

Not simply Bitcoin is related with blockchain technology. One would be mistaken to believe that Bitcoin is the only kind of cryptocurrency available. In reality, Bitcoin is only one of hundreds of current applications that employ blockchain technology.

Another open software platform built on the Blockchain is called Ethereum. It enables the creation and introduction of applications with a decentralized architecture.

Contrary to popular belief, Ethereum and Bitcoin are not exactly the same. The fact that both Ethereum and Bitcoin are public, distributed Blockchain networks unites them. But it should be highlighted that their main differences are in terms of skill and intent. One specific implementation of Blockchain technology, based on a peer-to-peer digital currency system, is Bitcoin. Online Bitcoin transactions are possible thanks to this method. All transactions conducted using Bitcoin on the site are recorded in the blockchain. When it comes to the Ethereum blockchain, its primary utility is allowing the platform's decentralized applications to execute their source code.

Miners are searching for Bitcoin on the Bitcoin network. Ether is the name of Ethereum's cryptocurrency coin. The goal that miners strive towards is this. The network runs on ether. On the Ethereum network, developers utilize the tokens to pay for any services or fees. The token may be used by individuals as a digital asset that can be traded.

The program must be installed on at least a few thousand computers for Ethereum to function since this is what fuels the network. The Ethereum Virtual Machine (EVM) is a program that runs on each computer in the network, sometimes referred to as a node. The Ethereum Virtual Machine (EVM) may be conceptualized as an operating system that understands and runs applications created in a programming language unique to Ethereum.

Ripple

The foundation of bitcoin technology is decentralization, as was already explained. However, ripple follows a more conventional strategy. By integrating blockchain technology, it gives the banking concept of SWIFT transactions a much-needed boost.

Currently, transmitting conventional currencies over SWIFT involves a number of middlemen and takes a few days. Compared to what Ripple offers to provide, the procedure is less safe and riskier. On the other side, ripple offers quicker and more affordable transactions that are powered by a single coin, XRP. Over 100 banks are now cooperating with the ripple team on a global scale, including ATB Financial, CIBC, UBS, Standard Chartered, etc.

Monero

With the aid of Monero, users may send and receive money without a blockchain transaction being visible to the general public. By default, every Monero transaction is private. Monero checks all the criteria if your primary concern is privacy. The money is intended to be completely untraceable and anonymous. This extends to their development staff, which, in contrast to other currencies, lacks a CEO or other visible personality.

To enable untraceable transactions, Monero also employs "ring signatures," a unique kind of encryption. Due to this, people might receive money without being able to determine who sent it. Depending on how you feel about anonymity, you can perceive this as either a plus or bad. Along with the buyer and seller's identities, the transaction value is also hidden by the ring signatures. In contrast to Dash, Monero has always been open source, allowing anybody to inspect the source code for complete transparency.

The cash is a favorite of the dark web because of its anonymity. AlphaBay, a Darknet marketplace, used both Monero and Bitcoin to handle transactions before it was shut down. On the network, people exchanged anything from illicit substances to weapons to credit cards that had been stolen. Monero is a preferred cryptocurrency among ransomware hackers due of its anonymity.

It is unclear if Monero will expand into more legitimate uses like hiding one's real net worth or whether it will be the preferred currency of more illegal enterprises, preventing it from becoming widely used like other currencies. When looking to make money from the possibility of broad adoption, speculators may be able to take advantage of this uncertainty.

Litecoin

Litecoin, the initial altcoin, has stood for unglamorous but steady development in a cryptocurrency market driven by hype and significant boom/bust cycles. Litecoin was introduced in 2011 with the goal of being "the silver to Bitcoin's gold" and addressing the issues that Bitcoin had at the time. As a result, many analysts have labeled it the "low-risk coin." Litecoin's coin limit is 4x that of Bitcoin's at 84 million coins, making it too, a deflationary currency.

A block takes 2.5 minutes to construct, which is less than half the 10 minutes required by Bitcoin. Before Ethereum's surge in 2017 Litecoin had long held the title of second-largest cryptocurrency by market capitalization.

Due to its quicker block generation time than Bitcoin, Litecoin has a significant edge over the latter in terms of transaction volume support. Because there are no transaction fees involved, businesses may send and receive money very quickly. Bitcoin, on the other hand, would cost more and take four times as long to complete the same transaction. Aside from having one of the most active development teams among all cryptocurrencies, Litecoin also underwent a series of cutting-edge improvements, becoming the first cryptocurrency to use Segregated Witness (SegWit) technology. The benefit of having the second-most secure blockchain after Bitcoin itself is also provided by this for the currency.

The adoption on significant exchanges is another benefit for potential investors. In March 2017, Coinbase became one of the largest cryptocurrency exchanges to offer buying Litecoin using fiat money, which was fantastic news for investors in the US and EU. In terms of market behavior, generally speaking, gains and declines in the value of the currency follow a similar pattern for both Bitcoin and Litecoin. To diversify their portfolio, many investors pick Litecoin as an extra cryptocurrency to Bitcoin.

For those who are interested in mining, Litecoin has a much simpler algorithm, which lowers mining expenses and entrance hurdles. While Bitcoin uses the SHA-256 algorithm, Litecoin uses the Scrypt algorithm. Practically speaking, this has the most impact on decreased mining costs since Scrypt is less demanding on graphics processing units (GPUs). In 2017, Bitcoin mining is no longer a feasible choice for amateur or home-based miners, however Litecoin mining may still be profitable, especially when taking into account the cost of power in developed nations.

The currency was also a victim of a Chinese pump and dump fraud in 2015, in which investors gathered 22% of all the coins in circulation before selling them. Litecoin's critics have slammed the coin for being "just another Bitcoin with no innovation."

Factom

Like Ethereum, Factom explores applications for blockchain technology beyond monetary exchange. Factom claims to achieve the same with massive blocks of data by offering an unchangeable record system, in contrast to Ethereum, which is predicated on two-way verification and guaranteeing that contracts are unbreakable.

Businesses and governments would be able to give a history of data without change or loss if this were to happen. Legal applications, business accounts, health records, and even voting systems are some examples of practical uses for this. Just try to picture a world where rigging elections or accounting scandals like Enron were literally impossible.

Factom, like other blockchain-based initiatives, cannot be changed since the network is controlled by a decentralized organization. Independent of one another, millions of users jointly control the network. The same cannot be done with data held by a whole network, while data owned by one individual is vulnerable to maliciousness, hacking, user mistake, and manipulation.

Factoids are the "currency" of the Factom system in terms of investment, much as Ether is to Ethereum. These

Factoids are worth more the more apps that are produced utilizing Factom. To supply blockchain-based administration software projects for Chinese cities, Factom has already signed a contract with consultancy company iSoftStone. Plans for auditing and verification services are part of the agreement.

According to Factom CEO Peter Kirby, the technology will enable the creation of an entirely new category of trustworthy and impenetrable corporate systems. This might apply to any system where maintaining records is crucial, such as insurance, financial services, healthcare, or real estate.

Scalability and greater technological adoption are frequent concerns with Factom, as they are with other blockchain technologies. The team's ability to operate the system at a steady profit in the future—or if the technology will result in a race to the bottom in terms of price—is the second major disadvantage of Factom investment.

Golem

Golem is a cryptocurrency token built on the Ethereum network. The value of the currency, dubbed by some critics as the "Airbnb of computing," is based on the applications that may be created with it.

The Golem Project's creators refer to it as a "supercomputer," with the ability to connect with other computers for a variety of uses, such as scientific research, data analysis, and cryptocurrency mining. For instance, if your computer has unused power, using the Golem network, you can rent that power to someone else who needs it (hence the Airbnb comparison).

The ability to monetize users' idle computing power is a no-brainer in theory, but it remains to be seen how the technology will be used in practice. The Golem team's lack of marketing exposure also appears to have hurt the coin's value recently. The inability to purchase GNT with fiat currency (such as USD) is another disadvantage for the mass market.

The Golem Project has a very real chance of fizzling out into nothing, but on the other hand - there is tremendous potential for large future gains with the price of a coin still under $0.30. It should be noted that the technology is still very much in the early development stages and as of August 2017; the team is still looking for alpha testers for the project.

Please provide an honest review of this book on Amazon if you are enjoying it.

Please sign up for the newsletter if you'd want further details regarding the publication of new books:

How to manage your bitcoins

The so-called wallet, also known as the electronic purse, is a piece of software or a file that houses a list of private keys and allows you to manage your bitcoins. The cryptographic data known as a private key enables users to transmit and receive bitcoins.

Making a payment is as easy as sending an email; all you need to do is put down the recipient's information, choose the appropriate amount, and complete the transaction.

To receive a payment in Bitcoin, all you need to provide someone is their address, which is made up of 27–34 alphanumeric characters (apart from the digits 0 and the letters I and L). For instance: 1dice8EMZmqKvrGE4Qc9bUFf9PX3xaYDp.

There are 51 characters in a private key.

A person with access to a wallet's keys has the ability to control it, and as a result, steal the bitcoins stored within. The paper wallet is an alternative kind of wallet that allows you to manage your money by simply writing or printing the private key (or keys) and the public key on a piece of paper. Of course, you must take precautions to ensure that no one may spy on you or steal the paper. The deterministic purse, which enables you to create an endless number of keys from a single seed code, could be a useful way to reduce the danger of theft. When using the deterministic purse, you only need to keep the seed code since the keys and addresses will be produced from it in the future.

How can I get bitcoins?

One approach to get bitcoins is to sell goods or services and receive payment in bitcoins. The second is to use an exchange service to buy or sell bitcoins for dollars or euros. The third method of obtaining bitcoin is by taking part in the protocol for transaction validation and network insertion, where you will get a tiny fee for each transaction that is accepted. In reality, bitcoins are created according to a straightforward rule: per 10 minutes, a certain amount of bitcoins must be created and then added to the peer-to-peer network via a process known as mining, which verifies user payments. First to crack a suitable cryptographic game wins.

Block system and block chain

Every time a transaction is made in the Bitcoin system, a distributed server dates it. This server generates the hash of the item, or piece of information, and adds it to the Block Chain, which serves as a public record of all Bitcoin transactions.

Every payment is tracked by one or more transactions, which are then collected in blocks to create the Block Chain.

Because each block has a control code that relies on the one before it, they are all somehow related to one another. As a result, it is impracticable to alter one block without altering all earlier blocks as well. Starting with the creation and activation of the system, the control codes set the chronological order of the blocks in a certain way.

1.1 Definition. As an abbreviation of the English phrase "number used once," the term "Nonce" in cryptography refers to a random number that can only be used once.

In order to prevent the reuse of data from previous connections, authentication techniques utilize nonces. Blocks that include control codes make use of nonce values.

Why did the blockchain start out?

Young Americans were dying far from home in a war they did not comprehend in 1968, French students were protesting the consumer culture, and people were starting to demand liberal self-management systems independent of boss-imposed regulations. In this ecology, appealing notions for the protection of property and pure capitalism—capitalism that was directed by human choice and sought social justice via the deliberate allocation of resources—began to take form, removed from the bloodshed of the previous revolutions.

These notions, which formed the basis of the collaborative economy as we know it today, were written down in the years that followed.

Currently, Blockchain technology is what makes these concepts a reality.

Blockchain technology enables people to communicate with one another without a central authority that is enforced by the system.

In other words, Blockchain does not need major enterprises, governments, or other institutional bodies to control interpersonal interactions. Blockchain is an intelligent arbitrage system that gives all inter-person transactions legitimacy and confidence via a fair consensus method.

So, the issue is no longer what is Blockchain, but rather, can the present market absorb the Blockchain movement, much as the May '68 youth movement was absorbed by the consumer market it was attacking?

WHAT IS THE BASIS FOR IT AND HOW WAS IT CREATED?

Although blockchain is a sophisticated technology, it may be easily understood.

Imagine a world with 1,000 computers, each in the house of a typical person, a family, or a student—people who are strangers and who make their own choices. Let's say these machines are a part of a Blockchain network, for now.

You must be asking why they are a member of the network. Quite simply, people do it for financial gain in addition to believing in you. Every time data or virtual currency is sent, a modest fee is paid to one of these machines.

Now that we know why a computer is used by a public Blockchain network, let's proceed with the scenario where someone chooses to send a Bitcoin transfer to pay for theater tickets. Well, the computers also verify the transaction in addition to sharing the fee money that the transfer costs.

Let's use the following scenario to illustrate how blockchain validates actions and the advantages of information distribution: If I transfer information to 1,000 computers, those machines store that information.

A complex arbitration system based on game theory would cause the remaining 999 computers to tell the changed computer: "you made a mistake, the information is 1," and the changed computer would again give the correct information, i.e. 1 if someone attempted to change the information of one computer and said that the information is 0 and not 1.

In regards to the case of the ticket purchase, the a thousand computers confirm that a transfer of value X from my account to the theater's account was made. Someone would need to "change the mind" of a thousand computers in order to alter or breach this information. No amount of computer power can compare to the transactions confirmed by more than 40,000 nodes. This is the strong base on which the Blockchain is constructed.

WHY ALL THE BLOCKCHAIN CRAZE?

Isn't it alluring to cling to the allure of a technology that makes it possible for anybody to establish a bank, that democratizes profits, and that gives people hope that they may escape a system that no longer serves as a moral compass?

Public Blockchain networks are impervious to fraud, hacking, and corruption. How am I supposed to restrain myself from having better-functioning world dreams?

Because for many individuals, Blockchain is still the Holy Grail or even, for some, an exercise in alchemy, there is a significant difference between the conceptual Blockchain and the actual Blockchain. Dreaming is reasonable and normal, as is hoping.

Realities and aspirations must be in harmony.

Websites of Value

The "Internet of Value," literally "Internet of Value," refers to those systems that enable the exchange of value over the Internet with the same ease as information is done today. Blockchain technology is a component of this complex and continuously changing universe.

The term "Internet of Value" refers to a network of digital nodes that exchange value among themselves using a set of algorithms and cryptographic principles that enable consensus to be reached even in the absence of trust on alterations to a distributed ledger that records transfers of particular digital assets.

Therefore, many galaxies or, more precisely, various platforms that facilitate the creation of Blockchain solutions, orbit inside this universe. The two main categories of these platforms are permissionless and permissioned.

- Without permission. Anybody may take part in the transaction validation process and can join the network as a node in a blockchain. Bitcoin and Ethereum are two of the most well-known permissionless cryptocurrencies, however there are many additional ones (more than 900).

- On the other hand, blockchains with permissions are distinguished by limiting network access to a small number of approved users and by delegating the validation process to a small number of actors. Hyperledger and Rope are two of them.

- This category includes certain "hybrid" systems, like Ripple, that, for instance, let anybody to join in the network but only a select few to handle transaction validation.

Blockchain technologies' qualities

There are several platforms that might compete to allow the Internet of Value, as we shall discover later in this guide: from Bitcoin to Ethereum, from Iota to Nano, from Zcash to Monero. There are already more than 1,000 platforms, and more are being created daily. Although each one is distinguished by unique settings, it is still feasible to pinpoint 7 universal aspects of Blockchain technology. Obviously, the first one pertains to digitization and the conversion of data into digital form. Here are the remaining six:

DECENTRALIZATION

To enhance cybersecurity and system resilience, data is distributed across numerous nodes while being captured.

TRANSFERS CAN BE TRACED

Each item on the register may be tracked back to its precise origin in every detail.

DISINTERMEDIATION

Without the need of trusted central organizations, or middlemen, platforms enable the handling of transactions.

INTEGRITY AND VERIFICATION

The register's content is readily accessible, clear, and observable by all parties.

IMMUTABILITY REGISTER

Data that has been entered into the register cannot be modified without the network's approval.

PROGRAMMABILITY OF TRANSFERS

Capability to plan activities that are carried out when certain events take place

Cryptocurrency Faucets

This may not be the most well-known or lucrative method to earn bitcoin, but it is a way to get a little amount without spending any money. These websites are known as "faucets," and they allow you to do basic tasks in exchange for a little payment in Bitcoin or another cryptocurrency. The majority of faucet websites are either focused on promoting virtual currency or increasing their traffic in order to sell ad spots. If the website's primary source of income is from advertisements, it could be prepared to give you a percentage of that income in exchange for your watching these ads and potentially doing some follow-up surveys. These faucets include BestFaucet, TopFaucet, BTC Clicks, and Bitcoin Aliens, as examples. The second kind of bitcoin faucets, which primarily work to promote digital currencies, would provide you little amounts of a currency as a risk-free trial without requiring you to put any money

up front. These websites often want to get you involved in the trading of cryptocurrencies, so they provide you with these examples to use as a demo and get familiar with the concept of utilizing cryptocurrencies. In addition, there are other bitcoin faucets where you may get money by introducing your friends to the website. These faucets include lottery and betting services. Users are often paid in Satoshis using faucets. One Bitcoin is equal to one hundred millionth of a Satoshi. They are rather modest, but depending on the exchange rates, if you have a sizable lot in your wallet, they may add up to something useful. The return won't ever come near to that of trading or mining, of course, but then again, this is a zero-capital activity, so don't expect to strike it rich. However, it may be your entry into the cryptocurrency world.
While visiting one or many of those faucet websites to make a few Satoshis would be a safe idea, you may also invest in setting up your own cryptocurrency faucet website. Your website's traffic

may rise exponentially if you create an alluring referral program and a generous payout plan for your users, which you can then sell for advertising earnings.

Using the Internet to Earn Cryptocurrency Payments

You may provide your services for a fee in Bitcoin or any other cryptocurrency via websites and mobile applications. These services include trying out online games, viewing films, completing surveys, and doing a variety of other little chores. Applications like Bituro, Coinbucks, and Bitcoin Rewards may be thought of as the bitcoin equivalents of websites that provide freelance services like Freelancer or Upwork.

There are other sites that are even more comparable to Freelancer and Upwork, allowing you to provide your talents there in return for bitcoin payments in a variety of disciplines including web development, content writing, etc. Two such websites are BitGigs and Coinality. You sign up for them, bid on tasks you believe you can do, and be rewarded in Bitcoin or any other cryptocurrency.

Considerations for Cryptocurrencies

There are many other cryptocurrencies out there that are equally worth paying careful attention to, even if Bitcoin's success at the end of 2017 shown that it is still the king of the hill. Other pertinent cryptocurrency kinds that are projected to see significant movement in 2018 are covered in great detail in this chapter. It is crucial to remember that this will only be a brief overview and that it is also crucial to stay current on your preferred cryptocurrency because things can change very quickly. The longer it has been since this book was published, the more likely it is that some of the information contained here is outdated. Any significant cryptocurrency exchange should provide the following currencies.

Ethereum

Ethereum is the most well-known cryptocurrency platform currently available on the market, after Bitcoin. Ether, the company's cryptocurrency, is mostly used for the direct payment of services for apps and smart contracts that operate on the Ethereum platform. Ethereum is primarily interested in providing as a platform for the development of blockchain and smart contract technologies, with ether serving as a convenient means to enhance interactions, while Bitcoin is almost entirely focused on person to person transactions. However, there is some speculative activity with ether as well, and as of January 2018, one ether is worth roughly $900.

A Bitcoin programmer by the name of Vitalik Buterin proposed in a whitepaper from 2013 that a programming language be added to the Bitcoin blockchain, leading to the creation of Ethereum. Buterin resigned his employment when his idea was rejected, spending the subsequent two years setting up Ethereum in preparation for its debut in July 2015. The virtual computers that operate these apps need ether to function, and they depend on gas or a fraction of a single ether to pay their operational expenses to the system as a whole. Every year, over 18 million new ethers are produced.

Be aware that Ether will convert from the widely used proof-of-work validation mechanism to a proof-of-stake validation system in early 2018. The new method will choose the next block's creator in a mostly random manner, with each validator (the substitute for miners) having a greater chance of selection the more involved they are in the system. Then, rather than being mined, blocks are considered to have been forged. For any quantity of ether, forgers will have the option to join the system. The chosen sum will then be effectively kept prisoner, and ownership will be revoked if they engage in unethical behavior. The usual mining incentives will subsequently be replaced by transaction fees for forgers.

While Bitcoin stole the show at the year's end, Ethereum had a very successful 2017. This was in large part due to the establishment of the Ethereum Enterprise Alliance, a group of Fortune 500 companies and blockchain startups committed to promoting the use of blockchain technology globally. By the end of 2017, the group had more than 100 members, up from only 30 at the beginning. The Alliance is actively developing a blockchain to better serve the needs of the commercial and financial sectors.

Smart contracts are recorded alongside transaction data in the blocks of the

Ethereum blockchain and are passed from node to node just like any other sort of data. As a result, nodes may see longer than usual upload delays due to the cumulative drag of all the smart contracts on the chain. Despite this, the Ethereum blockchain can only handle roughly 25 transactions per second, however this rate is anticipated to rise once the proof-of-stake method is implemented.

BTC Cash

The blockchain of Bitcoin uses outdated technology, which is one of its main issues. Although this is logical given that it was the first of its type, it has long had trouble handling the volume of transactions that its popularity has demanded. Additionally, despite the community's persistent efforts, the issue doesn't seem to be getting better any time soon. The single megabyte size restriction on blocks in the Bitcoin network is one bottleneck in the problem. The fact that the blockchain can only handle seven transactions per second at its most complicates matters further.

The most recent and straightforward solution to this problem to date is bitcoin cash. On August 1, 2017, a hard fork was introduced onto the Bitcoin network, resulting in its creation. Its block size limit is eight times larger than that of the conventional Bitcoin blockchain, which is the main distinction between the two. Due to this, the blockchain infrastructure can handle eight times as many transactions without any more labor being required.

The implementation of the Bitcoin Improvement Proposal, which became effective in July 2017, led to the creation of this hard split. With this idea, the blockchain was tricked into believing that the data in the conventional blockchain blocks was less than it really is. The community segment that has since joined Bitcoin Cash believed that doing so would just postpone dealing with the cryptocurrency's real issue, which is the platform's fundamental incapability to scale. Furthermore, the BIP helps to support people who choose to see Bitcoin as a speculative investment rather than a legal tender.

As a result, Bitcoin Cash has already earned a reputation as the cryptocurrency that people who truly want to spend their money prefer. Up to block 478558 and its first distinct block, which is block 478559, it retains all of the transactional information from the original blockchain. The Emergency Difficulty Adjustment method, which Bitcoin Cash began implementing at the same time, quickly made it roughly twice as lucrative to mine as regular bitcoins, but only on sporadic basis.

Up until November 2017, when the algorithm was revised to offer more stability, this amount of variability persisted. Despite the fact that it took the market some time to take notice of it, Bitcoin Cash has only gained popularity since its launch and is currently listed on several of the most well-known exchanges, including Kracken, Bitstamp, and Coinbase, where it can be seen as either BCC or BCH on the trading ticker. In December 2017, one Bitcoin Cash was valued around $2,500.

Ripple

At the end of 2017, Bitcoin was the sole cryptocurrency seeing growth that far beyond everyone's expectations, making it the talk of the town. Ripple (XRT) began trading in December 2017 at only $0.25 cents a unit, but by the end of the month, it had risen to more over $2.50. Since then, thanks to a price growth of 1,000 percent, it has overtaken the unshakeable bitcoin as the second-most lucrative cryptocurrency by market value.

Even more advantageous for its long-term prospects is the fact that its price surge wasn't caused just by the fluctuation Bitcoin was going through. Instead, it was a totally normal reaction to a variety of pleasant occurrences that all occurred within the same month. First, Ripple finished locking up its cryptographic tokens, greatly enhancing its security. A concentrated surge of demand from Asian markets kept the upward trend moving less than a week later. From there, a Tokyo-based business said that preparations were being made to establish a consortium that would more thoroughly investigate the many ways in which Ripple might be utilized to produce the first cryptocurrency debit card in history.

Ripple differs from the other cryptocurrencies on our list in a number of ways since it functions as a kind of payment network for financial institutions, significantly easing the process of settling transactions between various parties. There are now three main branches of ripple. The parent firm and source of new developments is Ripple Labs. XRP (also known as Ripple, which might be confusing) is the token that is transmitted in the transactions, and RippleNet is the payment network for the business via which Ripple (the money) is moved.

With the exception of the fact that XRP was not designed to be used as a transactional currency, the Ripple blockchain functions in a manner similar to that of all other blockchains. Instead, it was created as a tool to make it simpler for financial institutions to carry out a range of operations without worrying about currency exchange beforehand. This indicates that XRP might be seen as more of a form of settlement token than a fictitious currency.

Its transactions are mined differently as well since it does not handle transactions in a conventional manner. In particular, the mining process does not produce any new tokens since transactions are instead validated by a number of individuals to ensure that a consensus is maintained. 100 billion Ripple were produced at the moment its blockchain went live, with 60% of them still in the possession of Ripple Labs. These 60 billion are only utilized for settlement and are not included in the Ripple Market Cap.

Trading in Ripple is more like trading in the FX market than other kinds of cryptocurrencies since the speculative market that surrounds XRP has little impact on the success of Ripple Labs. Because the typical Ripple transaction clears in less than five seconds, Ripple attracts new banks every day because it allows them to move around much more swiftly than they could otherwise.

Litecoin:

A P2P cryptocurrency called Litecoin enables cheap, almost immediate transfers between accounts located anywhere in the globe. There is definitely a reason why this is beginning to sound like the Bitcoin sales pitch. In particular, Litecoin was designed from the beginning to be the silver to Bitcoin's gold. However, as Bitcoin's fundamental problems became more apparent over time, their friendship cooled, and today many people see Litecoin as one of Bitcoin's key rivals.

The fact that anybody may fork the blockchain and add whatever new feature to the technology they like is one of the most crucial aspects of the opensource nature of the Bitcoin and blockchain code. Thus, the Litecoin cryptocurrency was first made available to the general public in October 2011 and was developed by engineer Charlie Lee. In order to make it simpler for users to mine with existing hardware, Lee decided to shorten the block generation time, increase the total number of coins, and change the verification method to scrypt. Lee wanted to alter the blockchain's operation in a manner that, in his view, would be beneficial. He specifically wanted to shorten the time it took for a new transaction to be validated since he was already concerned about it.

Before November 2013, when the price of Litecoin quadrupled in less than 24 hours, there wasn't much speculative interest in the cryptocurrency. In the same month, its market value surpassed $1 billion. By the end of 2017, Litecoin's market worth has more than quadrupled since that time, coming to $2.5 billion.

The most significant advance offered by Litecoin, and the reason it merits your attention the most, is that it was the first of the top-market-cap cryptocurrencies to adopt the Segregated Witness (Segwit) technology. By reducing the impact of the existing size limit limitations on blocks in the blockchain, this technique helps to speed up transaction times. To do this, the transaction is divided into the data used for the transaction and the data needed to validate it. The blockchain then perceives the block as having a different structure when the verification data is returned to the end of the block. After then, the main section is tallied as usual, with the verification data only occupying 25% of the space that it would normally occupy.

The so-called lightning network, which contributes to faster transaction speeds overall, is another advantage of Litecoin.

Even though it is not yet ready for use, when it is fully implemented, it will create a sidechain where smaller and simpler transactions will be diverted, enabling them to be processed more quickly. It will also free up more primary power for larger transactions on the primary chain, improving the speed of those transactions as well.

Finally, it's crucial to remember that Lee, unlike the Nakamoto pseudonym, is still actively working to enhance the Litecoin blockchain when speculating on a particular cryptocurrency's future worth. Due to the fact that no one else has volunteered to take on this job, this also makes him the most active public face for the Bitcoin blockchain as a whole. When it comes to widespread adoption, having a face that the public can associate with the technology might easily prove to be a determining factor.

The Segwit protocol is now being promoted by Lee since it has taken some time for Litecoin users to embrace it as a standard practice. Mass adoption is now at the top of his list of goals going forward since it is essential to the effective launch of the Lightning network. As soon as 75% of users indicate that they support the chain, the update will become live across the whole chain.

Ethereum Smart Contracts

Because bitcoin was the first cryptocurrency, blockchain was first developed for use with it. But when Ethereum came along, a technology had been developed that would enable the creation of smart contracts. The cryptocurrency that will concentrate on peer-to-peer transactions is Ethereum.

Due to the fact that the method is the same regardless of the blockchain you are using, you will learn how to construct an Ethereum contract in this chapter.

Additionally, you will learn how to examine your contract so that you can make sure it is created according to your specifications before it is uploaded to the blockchain and put into use.

An example of a smart contract in the insurance sector

Definitions

You will need to understand a few terminology before you can publish your contract to the blockchain for usage.

Public key cryptography: a two-part scheme will make up the public key. Additionally an open key, the private key. A virtual signature will need to be created by each person to mark all of their blockchain work. Users must make a copy of their keys since they cannot access their accounts without them, therefore doing so is essential. Additionally, there won't be any external access to them.

Ethereum virtual machine: Smart contracts will be created using the proper blockchain infrastructure.

Dapp: smart contracts that are created and listed on the Ethereum market will be utilized with this decentralized application. Either a central server or Ethereum nodes will power the Dapp.

All transactions made on a cryptocurrency network will be recorded in a public ledger called a blockchain.

The digital money utilized with Ethereum is called ether. One ETH, also known as ether, will be equivalent to 65 cents in US currency.

beginning the deal

Although it is not necessary, it is advised that you create your own Ethereum node when creating your contract, even if you do not intend to utilize it. You will be able to connect to the full Ethereum network when you utilize a node. This will feature Python, Haskell, C++, and Java utilities for Ethereum.
The solidity tool, which is currently a programming language, will be the main programming tool. When utilizing the.se

or.sol extensions, it will be the Ethereum version of JavaScript. It will also be necessary to use a compiler. Make sure you have the C++ library so you can create your contract with all of the necessary tools. Installing Solc is no longer necessary after you download C++. You may use Cosmo as an alternative, or you can utilize the online version that is accessible at etherchain.org. Web3.ja, an API program that creates dapps, is the last item you will need. A solidity contract will be submitted to the network after it has been created. After that, web3.js will be used to recall the contract. Therefore, you will now have the choice of creating web apps that will correctly interact with your contracts.

It is necessary to utilize the distributed application framework known as Truffle if you want to benefit from an existing framework. The suggested option for utilizing a simple program that you can comprehend while enabling a greater focus to be put on the individual code is truffle. You must utilize blockapps.net if you don't want to use your own node. Another API you can use to simulate dealing with a node for testing reasons without actually using your own node is this one.

Contract specifications will differ significantly, which implies that each contract will need certain factors in one way or another. Consider the fact that if an event happens, the outcome will be recorded in a log and a contract will be created, but it won't change how the trade functions. At the same time, there is a function that will change the values that were set before the contract was activated in order to change the yes and no status of the contract. When certain circumstances are satisfied, the transfer will be made from one account to another thanks to this feature.

Your wallet's location and whether the contract can access it will be determined by the contract's address, which will keep the wallet address distinct from the creator address. The size of the contract will be the next variable; the smaller the contract, the better it will function. Additionally, a smart contract will be able to access the oracle's data by utilizing a public variable that will ultimately decide whether or not the data needs to be consulted and from whence it will be coming.

Other factors you should think about

You must review the data you are working with as you draft contracts to ensure that you have included all the information necessary for the contract's requirements to be fulfilled. The general structure of the file you are altering will be decided by a list of factors that you will have at your disposal. This information will typically be kept in a 2-x-n mapping sequence. The number of completed transactions will be N, along with the particulars associated with each transaction.

Include the definition for two distinct struts while keeping the result in mind. The amount of the transaction will be in this strut as the first one will include information about the individual who initiated the transaction. The data for storage and any other information required for correctly mapping the contract will be held in the second strut. You must describe the database you are using with this strut in order for it to automatically label the contracts using the template you have generated.

After creating the template, you will describe the functions that will be used often and the prompts that will enable it to do the chores that need to be done every day. The owner of the contract will get the appropriate transactions. It was originally suggested that this concept be expanded to encompass the restrictions that the transaction would impose, the contracts fund account, and the applicable conditions.

An individual ID that is related to that contract and will be maintained in the area designated for that record will be used to identify the investor's activities. The system will have designated this space in advance so that it can keep track of all the contract outcomes in one location. The final deal will be created if a deadline has been set for the transaction. In order to prevent the contract from being repeated, this will then set off the final action, often known as the suicide action.

The user will now have the chance to decide what they wish to do with the money they have received. After the contract has been submitted, these outcomes will then be evaluated. You will be included in the investor category of a fake contract. To ensure that the agreement will respond the way you want it to, you must go through the steps of engaging with it.

correct execution

As you already saw, if you are not comfortable putting all of your information together before you test your code first, Truffle will be the programming approach that will make your contract more manageable. Truffle will use a Java framework to verify the contracts' scenarios as part of the authoring process. Keep in mind that, assuming everything in the contract is written properly, it will only take 10 seconds to verify the transaction. As you test your code for your contract, it is crucial that you keep time in mind.

In order for a new node to be established before the truffle program is launched, you must have access to the window on the console you are writing your smart contract on. When you issue the command, it will install truffle and trigger a spawn in the fundamentals of the smart contract's init. By compiling all the code and testing it for deployment issues, the code may be tested.

what takes occur next

Using the online Solidity compiler available at etherchain.org/solc, the contract's code must be formatted once it has been created before it can be added to the blockchain. Once your code has been prepared, you may submit the contract by spending a little amount of ether to get a signature box, where you can put your private key to identify the contract as being yours. The findings will then be sent to you through an ABI and the blockchain address where the data will now be kept for the duration of the contract.

The contract has to be deployed using truffle when everything has been built and updated. To access a new directory, you must launch the truffle console and use the init command. A new index will be built, and it will give the contract a .sol extension. In order to add the contract to the location designated for it, you will now access config/app.son. To deploy truffle at the root level, all you have to do now is restart your application and issue the tesrpc command. However, the blockchain should already have your contract active.

A user interface must be developed once the contract has been generated so that you may interact with the arrangement in real time. The dapp will be within a database with an HTML-based front end and be directly connected to the Ethereum network. The dapp will integrate truffle into a comprehensive network with CDN access if you are using truffle. The UI of the Dapp will be developed in a manner similar to that of websites.

Different frameworks will assist in the development of your dapp, making it simpler for you to manage. As you can see from the foregoing, you will have the choice of employing the truffle as a tool, but this is not the only one you may utilize. Although you will also be able to utilize Embark, the truffle will be the most user-friendly development tool for making your dapp.

Using truffle will result in the creation of a smart contract. However, it is crucial to be aware of the alternative possibilities available to you so that you may choose the application that is perfect for you after doing your research.

When dealing with dapps and smart contracts, Truffle will be an application that does the majority of the work for you.

Your contracts may be made accessible in the JS code of your choosing with the help of the Embark application. Additionally, Embark will make it such that any adjustments to your contract will be tracked. If this happens, embark will immediately redeploy your contract and dapp if necessary.

Dapp development

Use truffle when building your dapp as it will automatically compile your user interface once it is up and running. The truffle director has to be marked as an app so that it will gather the contacts the next time it is used. Additionally, it will save any new modifications in the build folder, where the truffle program may access them in an emergency.

The directory has to be marked as an app to begin with in order for it to locate the background pictures and JavaScript code that will be connected to the stylesheets and indexes. Depending on what you require, you may choose to immediately add the code to the already-existing file in order to gain the front-end UI option, which will quickly get your contract up and running. There is a section in the app.js file that, when opened, displays a welcome from truffle in the developer console. There will be a list of current commands when you first access this console.

When considering instructions, you should consider how to build a function that can be called each time a page loads. You will need to add a window using the window.onload code in the app.js file in order to do this. If you do this successfully, the console browser will display a variety of account information. Finally, a test will be used. Use the Conference.js function to check if the output is functioning as you want it to. Your production should be the balance, and whenever the crisis is postponed, the balance will rise.

You will test the outcomes using your node or a sample node that will give you results in real time after creating the app.js and index.html to match your demands. Please take note that the results won't be ready very fast. To make sure it will function properly, you should use the following code.

get --rpc --rpcaddr="0.0.0.0" --rpccorsdomain="*" --mine --unlock='0 1'verbosity=5 --maxpeers=0 --minerthreads='4' --networkid '12345' --genesis testgenesis.json

Two new accounts with the numbers 0 and 1 will be created. You must be aware that you will need both accounts in order to set distinct passwords for each report, which will result in the creation of a json test-genesis file under alloc on the account where your ether charges are held. The results will soon be added to your truffle application, allowing you to recompile the contract and re-deploy the results.

You will have the opportunity to construct a user interface for use with any dapp that quiet Cicero will develop. This application may be found at dapp-builder.metor.com. This tool will be used to generate HTML code that you may edit later for contracts built using jQuery, web3.js, or solidity. If you are uncomfortable with your level of competence when it comes to going through the procedure on your own, it won't go as easily as you would want it to. The stages you have previously seen above will be used in the UI that comes next. If it doesn't, there is a backup version that, in most cases, will make it simpler for you to utilize in order to solve your issue.

Even though the contract will be drafted at this point, you won't be finished just yet. You must evaluate the contract. When you look it through, you'll make sure the contract is properly drafted and doesn't require any adjustments.

If you look at the variables at the top of your contract, they will appear as follows:

Identify the public organizer;
mapping public registrants (address => uint) paid;
public non-resistance in Uint;
public quota in Uint

Address: Since this is the initial variable in your contract, the address should be the one from your wallet. When the constructor, conference (), is invoked, the address is set. However, the contract will often designate it as the owner.

You'll see that this is an unsigned integer, or uint. You must make every effort to keep things as compact as possible since there must be room on the blockchain.

Public: A variable that is called from outside the scope of the contract you construct will exist. The agreement will use it when dealing with a private modifier. However, you must make sure that the variable is set to public if you attempt to call upon it from web3.js.

Arrays and mapping: The arrays and mapping that Solidity uses, such as (address => uint), will have varied degrees of support. As registration fees were paid, an address will also be written down. These maps will have a more compact volume. So that their money are accessible afterwards, the mapping will be utilized to store the registrant who paid for them.

Additional information about addresses: This client node will store data about your account. There will be an array of 10 addresses accessible after your test has started.

Your initial account will have the designation "zero," and any transaction that doesn't specify the state will use that account as the default.

Contrasting the organizer address and the contract address, your contract will have a unique address after it is deployed that is distinct from the organizer's address. Your Solidity contract will be able to access this address. It will be used in the contract's refund ticket function with the address = this;

Suicide is a beneficial thing in Solidity since the contract will hold any money provided to it in case you commit suicide. The resources will be given to the deal's owner after using the destruct function. If this were not done, the money would eventually get locked up and would never be accessible. Therefore, it is essential that you include a suicide method in your contract so that, in the event that it expires, you may collect the money.

However, you will have the option of choosing a different address from the accounts array if you simulate a different party to the contract. As a result, you must use this feature to purchase a ticket.

Conference. purchase a ticket
Value: some_ticket_price_integer from accounts [1]);

Some function calls may be transactions: these deals will have a specified sender and a value that will be put within the curly brackets. Functions will be able to affect the state of your contract. After that, the money will be sent to the wallet's address. In order to retrieve values using Solidity, you may use the message. where the solidity functions are kept are sender and Ms.

Function public purchase Ticket
...
Participants made [msg. "sender" = "msg," value;
...
}

Events: When you are writing your contract, events will be an optional clause. Deposits will be configured to be transmitted within the contract so that the virtual machine can record them. They won't really accomplish anything, but it will be useful practice for you to keep track of all the transactions that have previously taken place.

www.ingramcontent.com/pod-product-compliance
Lightning Source LLC
Chambersburg PA
CBHW050253120526
44590CB00016B/2330